Wishing you so much
Happiness

WORDS BY PAM BROWN
ILLUSTRATIONS BY CAROLINE GARDNER

A HELEN EXLEY GIFTBOOK

*Happy dreams!
Happy wakenings!
Happy days!*

*M*ay your life have diamond days.

Every day is an astounding gift.
Open each eagerly.

I wish you things
to catch your heart in beauty,
in joy and in amazement.
Things that will make you shout
with laughter and stir you
to excitement.

May you continuously

be surprised by joy

May you find happiness
in a quiet, perpetual rejoicing
in small events.

happiness in

*B*e happy in small things.
They give great happinesses
the opportunity to
creep up on you, quietly.

small events

I wish you tremendous

love and

pleasures –

music, discovery and art

May you,
just once or twice
in your lifetime,
see something infinitely rare
and strange
and beautiful.

May every day to come
hold good surprises,
unexpected joys
– friendship and love and
quiet content.

I wish you friendship,
music, books,
a cat against your shoulder,
a scented garden,
evenings of content.

I wish you the beauty of silence, the glory of sunlight, the mystery of darkness, the force of flame, the power of water, the sweetness of air, the quiet strength of earth, the love that lies at the very root of things. I wish you the wonder of living.

May you today and always, share the wonders of the world

...everywhere you turn

May you find happiness
everywhere you turn.
In love and friendship
In music. Books. Art.
In mountains, oceans, deserts.
In woods and rivers.
In taste and scent and sound.

I wish you the happiness of
always having something to give:
– a surprise, affection,
– freshly-baked scones, paperbacks,
seedlings and apples,
– a fetching-in of shopping,
a hand with the tidying up,
a feeding of cats,
a finding of plumbers,
a listening ear
– comfort. Time.

May your touch
bring kindliness
and comfort

I wish you the joy
of always having someone
to share things with.

*F*ind kind, gentle friends.
Find fun friends
to share free, happy days.
Enjoy being with them.
May there always
be friends to share
your laughter,
your troubles and
your victories.

Take a chance!

I wish you the happiness of doing
what you do as best you can.
Of taking the risk of trying
of taking the risk of giving
of taking the risk of loving.

I wish you the ability
to notice little wonders –
a shell, a bird,
a single blossom,
a plume of cloud,
a shining puddle.
A constant source of joy.

wonders...

*B*right flowers! Beauty! Joy!

The very best of life!

That's what I wish for you.

Gifts

Most ordinary things – but seen
with a new perception.
Hedges laced with spangled
spider webs.
A dazzle of new leaves.
A splendid cat sprawled tiger-like
along a wall.
Gifts of every season, of
every time of day.
And given only to those
prepared to see.

...calm
...love

May you hold
…calm
when the world
is full of sound and fury,
…love.

If I could give you anything
it would be a quietness
at the very heart of your life
that would remain tranquil
and certain whatever befell.

I see! I

I wish you the happiness of finding you understand something that has till now defeated you, discovering something you never knew before.

I wish you the joy of mastery – of your own muscles, of a boat, of a bike, of a horse, of paint and canvas, analogue and digital, pastry, engines, calculus or French. Anything. Everything.

understand!

Surprise!

May you never cease
to be astonished and delighted by
happy surprises.

I wish you the happiness
of a deep and gentle night's sleep.

*May you
be able to say
"That was
a lovely day".*

I wish you quiet sleep,
dreams of easy talk with friends,
of roads leading to a reunion,
of sorrow comforted,
of hope restored.

After storms,
the sunlight.
After troubles,
happiness.
That's what I wish for you.

May every hardship
give you greater strength.

After storms,

after sorrow

I wish you the discovery
of what you are really good at
and what you really want to do.
And that you'll have the courage
and the luck that make
those dreams come true.

I wish you
the happiness
of finding something
you can do well
– anything.

May you find happiness
in things learned and done.
In discoveries.
In hope.

I wish you all good things –
especially the gift of
being able to let go.
Learn from sorrow and mistakes.
Then go on.

I wish you...
...the courage to choose the difficult.
...the will to unravel the complex.
...new skills, new insights,
new adventures.

I wish you all good things,
But most of all,
whatever happens,
Believe in yourself and go on.

love that is
shaped

To fall in love is only a beginning.
The true joy of love
is only shaped by time.
I wish you that discovery,
that happiness.

by time

Fly higher,
Fly further...
FREE!

Fly free. Fly high and far.
There will be times
when much will be asked of you.
I wish you the courage and endurance
and the wisdom you need.
My thoughts are with you always.

*W*hat would I give you
if I had the power?
The chance to use your capabilities
wisely and well
– to make a difference to the world.
...Promises kept,
discoveries made, goals planned
and reached.
Courage to endure and grow.
Joy, contentment, love.
A life worth living.

courage!

Wherever

*T*here will be new beginnings –
a turn in the path – and the world
will be at your feet, another and you
will be passing through
a wooded ravine.
All along your way there will be
new things to see and taste
and smell and touch.
This will be your happiness,
your life.
My thoughts go with you.

Beginn

I wish you the happiness
of letting the past go –
and finding new beginnings.

ings...

*M*ay the coming years
bring you new hopes,
new adventures, new discoveries.

Helen Exley runs her own publishing company,
which sells giftbooks in more than seventy
countries. Helen's books cover the many events
and emotions in life. Caroline Gardner's
delightfully quirky and bright illustrations
paired with Pam Brown's insightful and beautiful
words create this stunning new range.

Caroline Gardner Publishing has been producing
beautifully designed stationery from offices
overlooking the River Thames in England since 1993
and has been developing the distinctive
new ranges for many years.

WHAT IS A HELEN EXLEY GIFTBOOK?

*Helen Exley Giftbooks cover the most powerful
range of all human relationships:
love between couples, the bonds with families
and between friends. No expense is spared in making
sure that each book is as thoughtful and meaningful
a gift as it is possible to create:
good to give, good to receive. You have the result in
your hands. If you have loved it – tell others!
There is no power like
word-of-mouth recommendation.*

For a complete listing of all titles and gifts, visit:
www.helenexleygiftbooks.com

Helen Exley Giftbooks
16 Chalk Hill,
Watford, Herts,
WD19 4BG, UK.
www.helenexleygiftbooks.com